With warm friendly thoughts.
Fondly
Cynthia Holt Cummings

Christmas Ribbons

poems by Cynthia Cummings

illustrations by Lisa Peterson Rye

Cynthia's verses and Lisa's illustrations
bring best wishes for a Merry Christmas
and a Happy New Year.

Christmas Ribbons

Save your Christmas ribbons
To tie in Julie's hair
A blue one for the sky above
And red for roses fair
Green will tell of Springtime
With robins on the wing
And yellow is the color
For all the songs they sing.
Save your Christmas ribbons
To tie in Julie's hair
Silver is for laughter
And all the dreams you share
Ribbons are like flowers
That in a garden grow
Their colors make a rainbow
Fashion Diamonds in the snow.
Gold is for the treasured jewel
But none can 'ere compare
With a little girl like Julie
Wearing Christmas ribbons in her hair.

Christmas for Buff and Roger

This year a little miracle
Will see your Christmas tree.
A little lad who's not quite one
Will crawl around your knee.

The tree will have a special glow
To welcome in the day.
Every present tied with bow
Will soon be torn away.

On the floor his little hands
Will reach for one and all,
The building blocks, the windup toy,
The Teddy and the ball.

Together you will play
With contentment in your heart,
For how could any Christmas day
Have a better start?

Oh count your blessings one by one
Be Thankful once again,
For Him who came so long ago
To bring Peace on Earth-Good will to men.

David Michael's First Christmas

Dear David. . . . it's Christmas
That special time each year
When hearts are filled with happiness
And greetings of good cheer;
And all the little children
Close their eyes in sleep
Awaiting Christmas morning
For secrets stockings keep.

Candy canes and jumping jacks,
Little black trains that run on tracks,
A bright red sled and spinning tops,
Boxes filled with candy drops,
Picture books with nursery rhymes,
Music boxes filled with chimes,
Popcorn balls and apples red,
A teddy bear, a dolly's bed,
Little toy soldiers straight and tall,
A bag of blocks, a bright blue ball.

It's Christmas, David . . . .
A time for merry laughter
A knock upon the door.
A little lad like you
Plays with toys on the floor.

A time to love each other
To say a little prayer,
To reach with tighter handclasp
For the treasures that we share.

A time to be so thankful
For the friends we hold so dear.
Oh, David . . . .it's so special
When Christmas comes each year.

What Christmas Is

Christmas is Touching;
Looking for love in the children's eyes;
Trimming a tree with holly and lights,
Placing a star up high --
Wrapping each gift with special care,
Bowing your head,
And saying a prayer.

Christmas Gift

This Christmas card, our gift to you,
Is brightly tied with ribbons red,
Inside we packed, the whole year through,
Some words of kindness that we'd said.

And in the songs we heard each day
That made our hearts feel light,
We put a note of each new one
Into the corners tight.

Then in the middle of the box
We found some space to spare;
And this we filled with happiness,
That each of you might share.

And so once more at Christmas time,
When homes are bright and gay,
We wrap our Christmas Gift to you
And send it on its way.

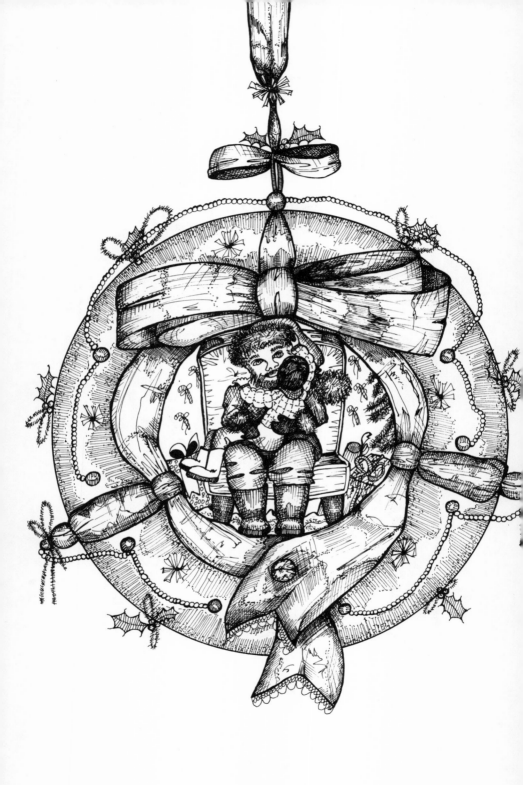

Christmas Wishes

I saw a Jolly Santa sitting in a chair,
And on his lap a tiny lad ran fingers through his hair.
Please Santa will you bring
A little doll for Sister Sue
And Mom would like a brand new ring
With stone of sapphire blue.

Now Dad would like an easy chair,
A place to sit when day is done;
And Santa please bring me
A little train to run.

I know your sleigh will be so full
When Christmas rolls round,
But if there's just a little space,
Bring smiles to wear on every face.

Christmas Star

Oh brightness of the leaf
When Autumn's all aglow
That thoughts could venture forth
To forests white with snow.

Above it all a brilliant star
To tell us all once more
The Glory of the Christ Child
As in Christmases before.

As though the yellow leaf
Reached up so high above
To give the Star its glory
and fill the world with love.

A Difficult Choice

A little girl's face pressed against the pane
Of the big store window that day.
Inside, once again, she saw the dolls
All in their bright array.
Oh, Santa, please bring me the one in red,
With her little fur muff of white,
She's just the right size for my dolly's bed
And I'll tuck her in at night.
Then suddenly the little girl
Saw the doll with real curly hair,
And she thought for just a moment
Of her tiny rocking chair.
'Twould be such fun to have a doll
With hair so soft and brown,
And she could sit in her little chair,
And rock her to sleep so sound.
But then far in the corner
Was a doll in snowy white,
Dressed as a bride for a wedding,
All on a Christmas Night.
Oh, the little girl was puzzled,
They were all so sweet and nice,
Especially the one wearing silver skates
To glide across the ice.
And there was a doll in a dance frock
Of the prettiest shade of blue,
Right next to the one in baby clothes
With a tag marked "Sister Sue".
'Twas difficult for the little girl
To choose for her very own,
The doll that Santa would bring Christmas Eve
To live in her world at home.

God's Mailbox

Dear Daddy;

It's Christmas and time to write
My own special letter to you tonight.
On the floor neatly placed under the tree
Are the pretty wrapped gifts for all to see,
And on the very tip top — oh up so far —
I've pinned a brightly gold-lit star.
The first letter I wrote when I was four
And Santa had brought me the doll from his store;
That was the year just before Christmas day
You told Mommy and me you were going away.
War had darkened the big land across the sea
And you went to help to keep our home free.
We missed you so Daddy — my Mommy and me,
And we waited and waited as each Christmas tree
Was trimmed with the lights so pretty and bright,
And your chair remained vacant each Christmas night.
Then the Christmas when I was finally eight —
Oh Daddy it was getting so very late —
And when you hadn't returned from the land so far
'Twas then Mommy told me about the gold star
That God had placed in his heaven so blue,
The star for my Daddy — it was just for you.

As each Christmas passes since I was four,
I sit down and write your letter once more,
And before I close my eyes in sleep that night
I drop it in God's mailbox, and soon it's in flight.

It reaches your star, and you read it right then,
And learn of the things that have happened since when
You left us that day so long, long ago
When the brown earth was covered with new winter snow.

The sweaters, so pretty when I was eleven,
Were gold for your star and blue for your heaven,
And the star cast its glow in the room that night
And reached out to touch your star so bright.
Tonight, Daddy, they tell me I'm a Junior Miss
And this letter I'll seal with a special kiss,
Add a dash of the perfume so sweet-scented I wear
And enclose a small lock of my brown curly hair.
In the closet my treasures, the ball and the top,
And the little store doll that Santa brought,
And on my dresser I plainly see
The picture of Mommy, my Daddy and me.
Oh the chair may be vacant, my Daddy, tonight,
But up in God's heaven, shining so bright,
Is the big gold star that will always last,
No matter the years that slip quickly past.
And in those years I'll always write
The letter for God's mailbox on Christmas night.
And as the sun sinks in the sky so blue,
Giving way to dark night once more anew,
I'll look in God's heaven and see shining bright,
The gold star God gave you one Christmas night.

A Mother's Christmas Prayer

In the twilight of the evening, sat a mother,
    hair of gray,
Rocking slowly in her chair, thinking thoughts
    of Christmas Day.
Now the house, so very quiet on this early
    Christmas Eve,
Soon would fill with happy laughter, children
    coming home would weave.
All year long, how she had waited for her
    children now to see
Once again in home of childhood gathered closely
    round the tree.
In the window, burning brightly, stood the yellow
    candles fair,
Sending out their Christmas message of a mother's
    silent prayer.
Please, Lord, make their trip a safe one, so that
    I may see once more
Happy faces of my children coming in my white
    front door.
Let me tell them once again of the glowing light
    that night,
As shepherds watching flocks looked up and saw
    the star so bright.

Christmas Prayer.

Christmases come,
Christmases go,
With the green fir trees
And the cold white snow.
Because a Child is walking there,
Peace for all
Is our Christmas prayer.

Christmas Thoughts
(Written in North Africa - 1943)

We are far away from you all tonight
In this land across the sea,
No Christmas lights to brighten our way,
As there are on your Christmas tree,
But shining high above us
Are the moon and the stars spreading light,
Sent by God's hand to comfort and guide us
On this, Our Christmas Night.

We know that you all may miss us,
But we hope and solemnly pray
That when Christmas time rolls round again
We will be home with you — home to stay.
So keep Christmas the same as you have before,
With laughter and merriment bright,
For even though a chair may be vacant,
We are with you there tonight.

A Prayer for Peace and Love

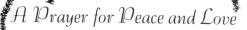

Green Fir Tree
With Christmas light
Reach out to all
The World tonight
And with the star
So high above
Spread the Prayer
for Peace and Love.

A Wish for You

Green Trees Candles Bright
Peace Be With You
On Christmas Night.

Christmas Music

I love the music for Christmas Day,
Carols sung in the same old way,
Voices of old and those so young,
Christmas Carols from every tongue.

Oh, for the music of Christmas Day,
Bringing the greatest joy
To every tiny little girl,
To every growing boy.

Music soft and sweet and clear,
Echoing from the voices here,
Filling air with music bright,
Music sung on a Christmas Night.

Christmas Glow

A cane, a doll, but that's not all;
There's love beneath the tree.

A book, a pen, now look again,
And in the star you'll see

The gold, the light that shines so bright,
That all the world may know

The joy, the peace that gives each face
That special Christmas glow.

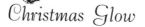

Christmas is for . . .

Christmas is for little boys
Toys beneath the tree
Brightly tied with ribbons
Tiny fingers hold the key.

Christmas is for little girls
With ribbons in their hair
Oh to see their eyes light up
As they descend the stair.

Christmas is for older folk
With wrinkles on their brow
Christmas is forever
Christmas is for now.

For The Children

May Christmas Peace
Fill all the land
With Children walking
Hand in hand
And may the Joy
Of Christmas light
Sparkle in their eyes
Tonight.

The Beauty of Christmas

I looked out my window in the darkness of night,
Saw the tree all aglow with its Christmas light,
Spreading cheer for the Christmas that soon would come,
With Peace here on earth to everyone.

And there, on the door of my neighbor,
Hung a wreath circled in light,
Like a halo of friendliness spoken,
For the coming of Christmas night.

The light-falling snow recovered the old,
With a brilliance of sparkling white,
And the sky overhead made the stars hidden bed,
All safely tucked in for the night.

And there on each roof was a blanket
Of downy new-fallen snow,
That covered the houses, with children
Sleeping ever so soundly below.

And the Mother and Dad before fireplace
Talked of a Christmas bright,
And the glow in the room was felt by both,
Of the coming of Christmas night.

I stood and looked at the beauty
That greeted my eyes in the night,
From a tree and a wreath lit with brilliance,
Reflecting their Christmas light.

One Little Hand Took Hold of Mine

One little hand took hold of mine,
"Come see the snow, it's Christmastime!"
Oh no not yet, I soon replied,
Not until each present is wrapped and tied,
And the tree is trimmed with colored lights,
And the star on top is glowing bright.

One little hand took hold of mine,
"Come see the snow, it's Christmastime!"
Oh no not yet, I answered again,
First come the shepherds and the three wisemen-
And the little stable will be dimly lit
Where Joseph and Mary will quietly sit
To watch over the babe with the star so bright,
To welcome in the Holy Night.

One little hand took hold of mine,
"Come see the snow, it's Christmastime!"
At last the day was really here;
The tree was trimmed
And the family near-
And the music of voices filled the air
With the spirit of Christmas beyond compare.

One little hand took hold of mine,
"Come see the snow, it's Christmastime!"

What Christmas is all About

One little light blinks on and off,
One little bell rings out,
One little hand holds onto yours,
And you know what Christmas is all about.

The Magic of Christmas

I'm counting the days until Christmas,
I'm watching the skies fall down
With snowflakes that come so gently
To cover the earth of brown.

I'm wrapping the gifts for Christmas
With Love and Joy in my heart
And I'm ending the year with magic
To give the New Year a start.

The trees that are tall and stately
In their winter coats of green
Will soon wear the colors of Christmas
Become part of the Christmas scene.

Lights will be blinking,
Bells will be ringing,
Voices will echo with song,
Oh for the magic of Christmas
To last the whole year long.

Be Thankful

Walk slowly thru the snow this year
Feel the cold breeze touch your cheek
Greet Neighbor with a Friendly Hand
Listen to the children speak.

Walk slowly thru the snow this year
Beneath a Starlit Sky
Be Thankful for your Happiness
As Christmas passes by.

Silhouette

Snowflakes slowly floating from the dense gray sky
Built drifts of downy white piled ever so high,
And as the tiny snowflakes all day kept falling,
Autumn left by the back door and winter came calling.
The valley was winter in white once more,
As I looked at its beauty from my own front door.
The fir trees beckoned with new weighted snow
That painted their branches now hanging so low.
Bright diamonds sparkled on the white-blanketed ground,
As the wind danced the snowflakes around and around;
The little birds took cover from the light falling snow
In the candy-tufted bushes nestled in a row.
Soon the daylight hours slipped into night,
And winter became a silhouette all in black and white.

The Christmas Elf

I saw him peeking through the door,
You know the Christmas elf-
He thought it was his duty
To trim the tree himself.

He wore a little suit of red,
His hair was snowy white,
And tiny little buttons
Held his shoes on tight.

He seemed to be so merry
For one so very small-
I wondered could he ever
Trim a tree so tall?

He circled round and round the tree
So quickly one could hardly see
The little buttons on his shoes,
But on each turn he'd stop to choose
A tiny bell, a candy cane,
And circle all around again.

Little ropes of tinsel,
Little wreaths with bows
Quickly left their places
And where do you suppose?

I watched with all my wonder
A sight my eyes could see
How a little elf at Christmas
Trimmed the tree for me.

The star it shone so brightly
Through the windowpane,
I hope that when it's Christmas
The elf will come again!

A Christmas Greeting

I've thought about Christmas,
The star and the tree;
The lights in the windows for all to see.
The red ribboned bows on presents galore,
The toys on the counter in many a store.

I've thought about Christmas
Both morning and night,
I've searched for a message
That would be just right.
I've thought about wishes
And greetings we send
As Christmas approaches
At each year's end.

And my heart over-flowed
With thoughts of Love
As I thought of the Savior
And the star above--
And so to each friend
Both near and far
We send you our Love
In the shape of a Star.

The Light of Love

Decorate this little tree
With love and Joy and then —
Give once again the treasured gift
Of Peace on Earth, Good Will to men.
Sit back and watch the branches glow
With light that only LOVE can show.

Christmas Joy

This Christmas may we wish you all
Some joys that come both large and small —
Warm sunshine on a summer day,
The Children's laughter while at play,
A rainbow that a sunset makes,
And courage that a new deed takes,
The autumn leaves with colors bright,
A star-filled sky on a winter's night,
The greetings from a new found friend,
A peaceful sleep at daytime's end.
Keep all the joys we send your way,
This is our Christmas wish today.

The Little Clown

He walked and he hopped
And he bowed way down
Such was the dance
Of the little clown.

He opened his eyes
And then closed them tight
The light of the star
Was glowing so bright.

He raised his hands
To touch the tree
And he thought of the splendor
The world would see.

He winked and he blinked
And he counted the toys
Marked with bright tags
For the girls and the boys.

Around and around
The tree he went
The minutes, the hours
Were quickly spent.

The clock was chiming
In the hall
And Christmas was ready
For one and all.

Ballerina

Tiny ballerina snowflake,
Under spotlight moon so bright,
Whistling wind your magic music,
Winter's stage you dance tonight.

The End

Christmas
Photos

Christmas
Photos

Christmas
Photos

Christmas
Photos

Christmas
Photos

Christmas
Photos

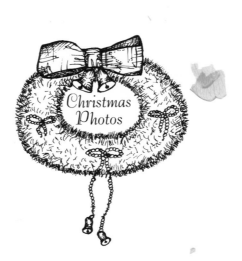

Christmas
Photos